Warfare Against Poverty

by Dr. Marlene Miles

Published by Freshwater Press

ISBN# 978-893555-98-3

Table of Contents

Foreword 7

Renunciations 11

Evil Vows 15

Evil Altars 17

Evil Arrows.. 19

Evil Bankers 22

Barrenness.. 24

The Blood of Jesus 26

Cages, Barriers 28

Evil Chains.. 30

Evil Covenants... 33

Debt.. 35

Demonic Stagnation 38

Divine Helpers 40

Favor 41

Garments... 42

Inherited.. 45

Lender Only 48

Opportunities.. 50

Possess My Possessions 52

Evil Programming.. 54

Redeemed from the Curse of the Law..56

Sickness & Disease..58

Slavery...60

Snail, Monitoring, & Familiar *spirits*......62

Evil spirits...64

Star..67

Strongmen...68

Evil Weapons..70

Wall of Fire..73

Wealth & Riches...75

Related titles by this author......................78

Other books by this author.......................79

Warfare Prayer

Against

Poverty

Freshwater Press

United States of America

Be glorified Father,

You are a warrior,

Mighty in Battle.

Exodus 15:3

We come to break the back of *poverty*

in the life of every believer,

in the Name of Jesus.

Foreword

Peace to you, in the Name of the Lord Jesus Christ.

I agree with Scripture regarding the poor: as long as there are unsaved, there will be those among us who are poor in *spirit*, and also poor in the natural.

But! Jesus died to redeem Believers from the Curse of the Law which includes being redeemed from sickness, death AND poverty. Jesus does not want us sick, dying, and/or poor. *Poverty* is not for God's children.

Warfare Prayer Against Poverty is for those still hindered by the curse of *poverty* even in their salvation. Sometimes what we desire to be simple is not simple, instead, it's complicated. We come out of sin by salvation in Jesus Christ. So, shouldn't everything in our life be "fixed" right then?

It's complicated. Even saved, sometimes, many times, we must be delivered with a mighty deliverance, fully into the promises of God. This is one of the reasons why there is prayer. It is one of the main reasons why we pray.

For those who are offended by prayers about *poverty* or money, I continue...

Believers are Redeemed from the Curse of the Law, yet there are still some sick among us. The Word says to call for the Elders to pray for the sick.

If we are saved, then why is there still sickness? The Word says to pray for the unsaved, that they may receive Salvation.

And we are to pray for those who *are* saved who have not received *full deliverance* evidenced by sickness and/or *poverty* in the Earth. It would be wonderful if when we got saved everything would just automatically be perfect. But it's not; it's complicated. So, we Pray.

Thank God if you do not need this prayer and may you continue to bless and be   blessed.

For any who are still offended:

The words of this prayer are *to* GOD and GOD alone. Let God hear it. Let God judge it. Let God answer.

We all work out our salvation with fear and trembling.

The remainder of this book *is a prayer*. So, open your mouth and boldly proclaim--

Renunciations

I declare, I renounce every kind of debt that is present in my life.

Evil load, unnecessary baggage, other people's *stuff*: I renounce you; I denounce you. You must leave my life, in the Name of Jesus.

Spirit of lack, I renounce you.

Spirit of debt, any and every kind of debt: I renounce you.

Spirit of insufficiency: I renounce you.

Spirit of poverty: I renounce you.

I renounce the *spirit of financial embarrassment.*

Spirit of shame, I renounce you. You must leave my life.

I renounce every evil power,

Water spirits in my generation that have swallowed my wealth, I renounce you.

I renounce the *spirit of Python.*

Python. I renounce you. You must leave me. I renounce you; I reject you with your *poverty*. You must release what belongs to me, in the Name of Jesus.

I renounce the *spirit of Leviathan.* Leviathan, I renounce you. You must leave me. I renounce you; I reject your *poverty*. You must release me and give back what belongs to me, in the Name of Jesus.

I renounce every sin, every financial sin I have committed. I renounce and I denounce you. I repent, in the Name of Jesus.

I declare, let the Blood of Jesus speak on my behalf, in the Name of Jesus.

I renounce every evil covenant I entered into with the Kingdom of Darkness, in the dream, by the Blood of Jesus.

I renounce every ancestral covenant that was entered into by my forefathers. I command you to be broken by the power of the Holy Spirit of God, in the mighty Name of Jesus.

I declare --I renounce every evil covenant of *poverty* in my family and in my generation.

I declare, I renounce every evil *pattern* of *poverty* in my family and in my generation. Behold, the Lord does a new thing in my life. Lord, let me do new things that tend to prosperity instead of old patterns that tend to *poverty*.

I renounce, denounce, and repent for my every work of the flesh, in the Name of Jesus. Pride, division, strife, lying, cheating, stealing, unjust balances, sexual sins, sins against godly covenants.

I declare, I renounce every covenant of witchcraft in my family and my generation.

I renounce and cancel every dream of *poverty* by household wickedness against my life. Vanish! in the Name of Jesus. I curse and cancel every wicked, evil, deceptive dream of *poverty* against me, in Jesus' Name.

I receive HOLY SPIRIT-inspired dreams from the LORD. I bind evil dreams away from me, in the Name of Jesus.

I smash every *poverty* dream to the ground, in Jesus Name.

Evil Vows

I renounce, denounce, and reject every evil vow and oath effecting *poverty* in my life, in Jesus' Name. Especially vows that I spoke.

I bind and cast out every negative word, every evil vow and oath, enforcing *poverty* upon my life, in the Name of Jesus.

Oh Lord, release my tongue to prosper; let the words of my mouth and the meditation of my heart be acceptable to you, oh Lord,

My Redeemer. I speak prosperity NOW. I am the righteousness of God in Christ Jesus. I prosper wheresoever the Word of the LORD speaks prosperity to me and over me.

Oh, Lord, take your place. You are the Lord of my life and the Lord of my family.

Oh Lord, take your place as a Lord in my life. I receive the power to be victorious in Jesus' Name.

The name of the LORD is a strong tower; the righteous rush in and they are safe. (Proverbs 18:10).

Evil Altars

Every witchcraft-sponsored *poverty*: die, in the Name of Jesus.

I declare, I renounce every covenant of witchcraft in my family and my generation.

Every natural and spiritual altar of *poverty* in my life, in my place of birth, working against my prosperity: Burn to ashes, in Jesus' Name.

Jesus came and died that we might have life and have it more abundantly, in the Name of Jesus. Thank You, Lord. (John 10:10b)

Every strength and power of environmental altars working against my life: wither and die, in the Name of Jesus.

Today I raise the altar of *continuous* prosperity from my destiny, in the Name of Jesus.

I send judgment against every evil altar erected against my destiny, in the Name of Jesus.

Evil Arrows

Every foundational arrow of *poverty* be removed by Holy Ghost Fire in Jesus' Name.

I paralyze all inherited arrows of *poverty*, in Jesus' Name.

Hear, O heavens, I'm dead to the covenant of *poverty*. I am alive to the Covenant of Prosperity, in Jesus' Name. The blessings of the LORD maketh rich and God adds NO SORROW with it. (Proverbs 10:22)

Every dart and arrow of *poverty* fired into my life come out with all your roots. Go back to your sender, in Jesus' Name.

GO BACK! GO BACK! GO BACK!

In the whole armor of God, I hold up the shield of faith which is able to quench every enemy fiery dart. Darts! Arrows! Go back to your senders! (Ephesians 6:16-18)

Every curse of *poverty* placed upon my family be consumed by Holy Ghost Fire, in the Name of Jesus.

Every arrow of *poverty* fired into my life by household wickedness, go back to your sender, in the Name of Jesus. For those who love cursing – let their curses find *them*, in the Name of Jesus.

I command the Thunder of God to break into pieces all evil arrows of *poverty* fired into my life or in my direction, in Jesus' Name.

Every foundational arrow of *poverty* be removed by Holy Ghost Fire, in the Name

of Jesus. I declare, I send them back to sender.

I paralyze all inherited arrows of *poverty,* in Jesus' Name.

Father Lord, shield me against any arrow of *poverty* in the Name of Jesus. I command every arrow to RETURN to Sender, in Jesus' Name.

I command the Thunder of God to break into pieces all evil arrows of *poverty* fired into my life, in Jesus' Name.

Evil Bankers

Every satanic banker representing me in the spirit world: fall down and die. I don't need you; I don't want you; I am represented by the Spirit of God, and Jesus Christ, in the Name of Jesus.

Every evil bank established against my destiny, be liquidated, be bankrupt, be permanently closed and shut down, by the Fire of the Holy Spirit, in the Name of Jesus.

Evil bankers, evil mortgages, evil loans, tempting evil financial deals, evil, pre-screened deals, and credit cards, I find you

out, I am not tricked; I reject every deception at every turn, in the Name of Jesus.

Every Egyptian *poverty* be terminated in the Name of Jesus; I am not your slave and I do not serve you in any way. The LORD released the captives out of Egypt with great possessions and wealth. Glory to God.

The frogs, the locusts, the Hiss of God that brings the flies, the bees and the stings are released against you, as God brings me out of Egypt and out of all slavery by His Mighty Hand, in the Name of Jesus.

I came out of Egypt, out of captivity to sin, sin bondage with great possessions and I claim those possessions now, today, right now, in the Name of Jesus.

Lord, thank You for delivering to me what I am do, based on Your Word, in the Name of Jesus.

I lay claim to my every blessing, right now, in the Name of Jesus.

Barrenness

Father, in Genesis, You told us to be fruitful and multiply. I bind every evil demon assigned against fruitfulness in my life, in the Name of Jesus.

Father, we are redeemed from the curse of the Law, let no barren be among us, in Jesus' Name.

I command the fruit of my life to come forward, in the Name of Jesus.

I speak to the womb of the Earth, do not smite me, but instead work in my favor, for my good, in Jesus' Name.

Father let living waters wash and let the rivers of Heaven flow to water any desert land in my life, whether it is the fruit of my body or the increase of my business, or the growth of my mind in education all to prosperity and to the praise of Your Glory.

I repent for my ancestors, Lord please forgive and do not hold any of their sins against me, by the Blood of Jesus. I am in Christ and Christ is in me.

I renounce and loose myself from every evil dedication of my womb, my mind, any part of my body, and my life to the dark world, in the Name of Jesus.

I take authority over all the curses emanating from breaking the vows made by my ancestors that is now affecting my fruitfulness, in the Name of Jesus.

Every devil associated with any broken, evil parental vow and dedication, leave now, in the Name of Jesus. Depart now, and never return. Forget my name and Lose my location.

The Blood of Jesus

I receive the sprinkling of the Blood of Jesus into every part of my life, in the Name of Jesus.

I plead the Blood of Jesus against every evil altar, whether household, remote, by known or unknown evil agents of darkness, erected against my destiny, in the Name of Jesus.

Problems, pack your stuff and leave my life now, in Jesus' Name.

Every satanic perfume that covers the Glory of God in my life, your evil stench be wiped off by the Blood of Jesus.

Wind of God, blow in freshness and newness of life; blow in prosperity and blow away all negative, *poverty* and filth, in the Name of Jesus.

My King shall reign, in the Name of Jesus.

Oh Lord, send your angels to dig out and destroy every evil root in my life, in the Name of Jesus.

Cages, Barriers

Every cage of *poverty*, be roasted to ashes in Jesus' Name; I refuse caged finances, I refuse caged life. I refuse caged Star. I refuse caged Destiny, in the Name of Jesus.

Every satanic barrier designed to hold me back from my desired and destined position be shattered into pieces by the Thunder Hammer of God, in Jesus' Name.

Every instrument of failure working against my advancement, I command you to fail, in Jesus Name.

I demand that the cover cast over me be lifted now in Jesus' Name so that my divine helpers can locate me.

Let every evil decree working against my potential be revoked, in the Name of Jesus.

My life, my destiny, reject and remove all marks of *poverty,* by Fire, in Jesus' Name.

Evil Chains

Network chains of failure rattling my life, melt off my life by Fire, in the Name of Jesus.

Chain the strongmen. Chain the devils, chain the demons, chain all evil powers in Jesus' Name.

Whom the Son sets free is free indeed: I am unchained, in Jesus' Name. (John 8:31)

You, anchor of failure weighing down my destiny, break, in Jesus' Name.

Every spiritual chain of slavery upon my life break by Fire, in the Name of Jesus. I

do not work for free; I know my value in the Kingdom of God, and in the earth, in the Name of Jesus. I am fruitful in all work, and I enjoy the fruit of my labor. Eccl 5:18-20

Every chain of inherited failure from my life, break by Fire, in the Name of Jesus. Everything God has assigned to me, everything I set my hands to-- prospers, by Jesus Christ, in the Name of Jesus. I can do all things through Christ which strengthens me. (Psalm 1:3, Philippians 4:13)

Holy Ghost, on my behalf, arrest every *spirit of poverty, lack, insufficiency,* and the *spirit of debt--,* in the Name of Jesus.

My God is El Shaddai, He is more than enough. There is no lack; there is no debt, there is only abundance, in Jesus' Name.

I dismantle every demonic opposition to my prosperity by the Blood of Jesus, in the Name of Jesus.

Every Satanic river of *poverty* and failure dry up by Fire, in the Name of Jesus.

Every altar of *poverty* prepared by my ancestors, in rebellion, ignorance or by deception, I break you now, in the Name of Jesus. BREAK! BREAK! BREAK, in the Name of Jesus.

Every witchcraft coven or assembly in my neighborhood be scattered by Holy Ghost Fire, in the Name of Jesus, never to be gathered or re-assembled again, in Jesus' Name.

Every *territorial spirit* working against my prosperity be chained with fetters of iron that cannot be broken, in the Name of Jesus.

I break every witchcraft covenant of *poverty* affecting my prosperity –break, in the Name of Jesus.

I break every curse flowing from every evil altar.

I bind the strongman and devil assigned to *enforce* the *poverty* curse in my life, in Jesus' Name.

Evil Covenants

Any covenant in my life that is strengthening the stronghold of *poverty* break, in the Name of Jesus. BREAK! BREAK!

Every curse, especially the curse of *poverty* resulting from evil covenants made-- I BREAK you right now, in the Name of Jesus.

I declare, by the Blood of Jesus, I break every covenant of witchcraft in my family and my generation.

Every covenant of *poverty* made by the living or the dead against my prosperity, break, in the Name of Jesus.

As a result of my prosperity prayers, I receive the mandate to enter into the Covenant of Wealth, in Jesus' Name.

Oh Lord, empower me with wealth that swallows *poverty* from my life.

Debt

You, mountain of debt programmed to put me into *poverty*, be cast away, in the Name of Jesus. I unravel your programming by the Blood of Jesus, in the Name of Jesus.

Every agent attached to too much work, too much effort, with little to no profit, be paralyzed, in the Name of Jesus.

I reject both the bread and water of affliction, in Jesus' Name.

I receive divine direction, in the Name of Jesus. Oh Lord, give me divine Revelation.

Oh Lord, let Your glory overshadow all the work that I do.

Oh God, arise and scatter every trap of *poverty* in my life, in the Name of Jesus.

Oh God, arise and disgrace every trap of *poverty* in my family, in the Name of Jesus.

The labor of my hand shall prosper, in the Name of Jesus. (Psalm 1:3)

Every waster of my prosperity be changed to efficiency or be gone, in Jesus' Name.

Every known and unknown opposer of my comfort, be paralyzed, in the Name of Jesus.

Anything planted in my life to disgrace me, come out with all your roots, in the Name of Jesus.

High interest. Late payments. Penalties. Easy credit rip offs: Devil, we know your games, and tactics and we no longer fall for them, in Jesus' Name.

I will not be moved, but every mountain of debt shall be moved, in the Name of Jesus.

I will not give up, but my problems will give up, in Jesus' Name.

All my problems surrender at the Name of Jesus. At the NAME of Jesus every knee will bow, (Philippians 2:10-11) AND stay bowed!!!

Demonic Stagnation

I reject demonic stagnation of my blessings, in Jesus' Name.

I claim big financial breakthroughs in the Name of Jesus. Lord, redeem the time, restore the years, in Jesus' Name.

Jehovah Jireh, the LORD my provider. El Shaddai – my God is the God of More Than Enough.

Every hidden devourer be exposed, show yourself, GOD rebukes the Devourer for my sake. Devourer, be bound and cast out in Jesus Name. (Malachi 3)

Jesus' work at Calvary releases me from every family pattern of *poverty,* in the Name of Jesus. (Galatians 3:13)

I refuse to allow my wealth to die on any evil altar, in Jesus Name.

My wealth: FIND me now, in the Name of Jesus.

I reject every prosperity stagnation and paralysis, in the Name of Jesus.

I possess all my benefits and possessions today, in Jesus' Name. (Numbers 33:53)

Angels of blessings, find me, locate me today and bless me, in Jesus' Name.

My pocket will not leak, in the Name of Jesus.

Every good thing, that my hands have started to build, they will finish it, in the Name of Jesus.

Divine Helpers

Let my divine helpers appear. Angels of Blessings, HERE I am—, in the Name of Jesus.

God of Providence raise divine capital for me, in Jesus' Name.

I occupy my rightful position in Christ, in the Name of Jesus.

Every delayed and denied prosperity, manifest by Holy Ghost Fire, in the Name of Jesus.

Magnets of prosperity, be planted in my hands, in my life, in the Name of Jesus.

Favor

Father, in the Name of Jesus, by the Fire of God burn away the covering cast over my face, head, life, hands so that I can be seen and also blessed.

Father, open heaven over me so I am favored and not rejected by people and opportunities will come my way, in Jesus' Name.

Garments

Garments of adversity, be removed from me now and burn to ashes, in the Name of Jesus, (Zechariah 1:1-5)

Garment of shame be removed from me now and burn to ashes. I call back my dignity and honor, in Jesus' Name. (Joshua 9)

I take off the Garment of Disfavor, by Fire.

Garment of wretchedness & poverty, moth-eaten garment, I remove you by Fire, in Jesus' Name. (Job 13:28)

Evil garments in the dream, I do not receive you; I reject you, in the Name of Jesus. Come off by Fire. Evil dreams, you are canceled by the Blood of Jesus!

Evil Garment of Disease; I am not ill, even though I feel the fiery darts and arrows of my enemies – I send them back NOW, in the Name of Jesus and I will NOT put on your evil garment.

I will not chase phantom diseases and symptoms in Jesus' Name. (Job 30:18)

By the stripes of Jesus, I am healed and made whole.

Ancestral, family & inherited garments don't hate the player; I don't hate my family, I hate the game. Devil I hate and reject your game in Jesus' Name.

Thank You, Lord, I put on the Garment of Prosperity.

I take off every evil satanic garment, by the power of Jesus Christ.

I break the power of every evil garment working against my life & command them to be destroyed, in Jesus' Name.

I release Fire to the worker(s) who sending that evil garment to me by the Power of the Holy Ghost.

Inherited

Every foundational *arrow of poverty* be removed by Fire, in the Name of Jesus.

I paralyze all inherited *arrows of poverty*, in Jesus' Name.

Every altar of *poverty* in my life, in my place of birth, working against my prosperity, burn to ashes, in Jesus' Name.

Let every parental mistake affecting my life, going back 10 generations on each side, be reversed, in the Name of Jesus.

Let the stubborn strongman of *poverty* in my place of birth, be paralyzed by Fire, in Jesus' Name.

Every covenant made at my birth, and in my place of birth, break, in the Name of Jesus.

I recover my placenta from the cage of wicked people, in the Name of Jesus.

Every altar of *poverty* in my life, in my place of birth, working against my prosperity, burn to ashes, in Jesus' Name.

Every evil hand that carried me when I was a baby, roast by Holy Ghost Fire, in the Name of Jesus.

I reject and send back every evil word spoken over me since I was born, up to now, in the Name of Jesus.

I break every *culture* of *poverty* in my life, in Jesus' Name.

Oh God, arise and let my head be lifted up, let the King of Glory come in and fight for me, in the Name of Jesus.

Who is the King of Glory? The LORD strong and mighty in battle; He is the KING of GLORY. Psalm 24

Let every evil seed of generational *poverty* dry up and refuse to germinate. Every evil root, come out, come out of my life, by fire with all your tenacles and roots, and die, in Jesus' Name.

I command the stronghold of inherited *poverty* in my life to be pulled down by the Blood of Jesus.

The BLOOD of JESUS separates me from all evil inheritance, in Jesus' Name.

Lender Only

From today, my portion in life has changed from beggar and borrower to lender and giver, in the Name of Jesus.

I am a Lender only and not a borrower.

I break the curse of *lack* in my life.

I break the curse of *insufficiency* in my life.

I break the curse of *poverty* in my life.

I break the curse of *not-enough* in my life.

I break the curse of Not-Enough-On-Time.

I break the curse of *debt* in my life.

I break the curse of needing to borrow, in my life.

I break the curse of monetary interest, penalties, surcharges, overages, and additional payments needed, in my life, in Jesus' Name.

I break the curse of evil and bad financial deals in my life.

Opportunities

Angels of God, Bless the Lord, and Praise His Holy Name!

Angels of Finance, you are loosed to bring me what has been apportioned to me out of my heavenly storehouse.

Angels of War – Warrior Angels, you are loosed to protect the provisions apportioned to me and being delivered to me so there is no delay, no theft, no destruction of what God says is for me. All, in the Name of Jesus.

Oh Lord. Create opportunities for my prosperity today, in Jesus' Name.

Thank you, LORD. Give me unction, energy, and strength to take hold of new opportunities in my life.

Angels of Opportunity, find me today, in the Name of Jesus.

Angels of Opportunity you are loosed to find and secure opportunities and establish an environment of favor around me and my life, in Jesus' Name.

Possess My Possessions

I possess my possessions. I grab by wallet back from every devil, demon, evil strongman, every evil principality, spiritual wickedness, Python, Leviathan, and all evil agents working under, or for Python or Leviathan, in the Name of Jesus.

In the Name of Jesus, I break every binding spell against me.

In the Name of Jesus, I undo, untie every rope, every knot set against me, my life, my finances, my person – every part of my person, every part of my life, in the Name of Jesus.

I am shielded by the shield of faith, and I send every knot, cursing and binding, encumbering curse back to the sender. Those who love cursing – enjoy your curses, in the Name of Jesus.

Devil, which part of this do you not get? I don't want you. I don't want to be in covenant with you. I will NOT be in covenant with you. I do not want your curses. I don't believe your promises, I do not enter into any deals or agreements with you. Get away from me, get far away from me – forget my name and lose my location, in the Name of Jesus.

Light has no communion with darkness. I walk in the LIGHT with JESUS CHRIST and devil--we are forever separated by the BLOOD--, the BLOOD of JESUS.

Evil Programming

Every evil machinery against my prosperity be destroyed, in the Name of Jesus.

Every evil programming, any evil assigned against me or working against me, be destroyed to ashes, in Jesus' Name.

Any computers assigned against me or working against me, and my prosperity be infected with God's viruses. Be locked with passwords that can never be recovered, smashed with the Hammer of God, set on fire by the Fire of God and

roasted to ashes, never again to be assembled, in Jesus' Name.

For the LORD is great. Holy is His Name. We ascribe all greatness, all riches, all strength, all honor to You, LORD.

Redeemed from the Curse of the Law

Jesus did not die for me to be in *poverty*. Devil, you are a liar!

I am redeemed from the Curse of the LAW by Jesus Christ. I am redeemed from spiritual damnation; I am redeemed from sickness. I am redeemed from *poverty*, in Jesus' Name. I shall not adjust to *poverty*, in the Name of Jesus.

Holy Spirit adjust my life to prosperity, in the Name of Jesus.

By the stripes of Jesus, I am healed, I am whole, my soul is at peace, and I am blessed, in Jesus' Name.

Oh Lord, take your place as a Lord of my life. I receive the power to be victorious, in Jesus' Name, Amen.

Sickness & Disease

Sickness, disease, and maladies in myself and/or every family member, costing me money needlessly--, I know this is one of the ways you steal money from humans. I bind you now, devil, in the Name of Jesus.

Phantom physical sickness and symptoms, causing me worry, fear and needless, expensive, time-consuming doctor visits that amount to, "Nothing is wrong with you," I bind you, in the Name of Jesus.

Hypochondriac spirit, I bind you, in the Name of Jesus.

By the stripes of Jesus, I am healed. Jesus sent Word and Healed me. I am made whole by the Blood of Jesus.

I curse the *spirit of poverty* that comes by chasing symptoms, sickness, and diseases with the curse of the Lord, in Jesus name.

I release myself from every bondage of *poverty,* in the Name of Jesus.

Slavery

I enjoy the work of my hands and enjoy the fruit of my own labor, in the Name of Jesus.

Every satanic banker representing me, in the spirit world fall down and die; I am represented by the Spirit of God, and Jesus Christ, in the Name of Jesus.

Every evil bank established against my destiny, be bankrupted and liquidated by Fire! in the Name of Jesus.

I bind up every avenue that the world uses to try to steal my money, or my family's money-- bad banks, bad banking. I break

the curse of bad banking off myself and my family today, in the Name of Jesus.

Every Egyptian *poverty* be terminated in the Name of Jesus; I am not your slave and I do not serve you in any way. And the LORD released the captives out of Egypt with great possessions and wealth. Glory to God.

Snail, Monitoring, & Familiar *spirits*

Every snail anointing on my blessings fall down and die, in the Name of Jesus.

Every power broadcasting, my goodness for evil be silenced, in the Name of Jesus.

Every *monitoring spirit,* or *familiar spirit* monitoring, watching my blessings and successes – be blind and be deaf and mute, in the Name of Jesus. Get out of my life! And do not tell any of my business to anyone else, ever!

I refuse to lock the doors of blessings against myself, in the Name of Jesus. The LORD opens the windows of Heaven and pours out blessings that there is not room enough to receive.

I am released from the *spirit of poverty* by the work of Jesus Christ at Calvary, in Jesus' Name.

Evil *spirits*

I bind the *spirit of laziness* in my life. Lord, forgive me and cleanse me by the Blood of Jesus. Give me a *spirit of action*, progress & productivity, in Jesus 'Name.

Any covenant in my life that is strengthening the stronghold of *poverty:* Break, in the Name of Jesus. BREAK! BREAK!

I renounce, denounce and reject all evil vows and oaths effecting *poverty* in my life, in Jesus' Name --, especially the vows that I, myself have spoken.

I bind and cast out every negative word, every evil vow and oath, and especially songs that I have sung over and over that are enforcing *poverty* upon my life, in the Name of Jesus.

Spirit of stinginess disappear from my life in Jesus' Name. I break the spirit of the closed hand, the closed, angry, fearful. un-generous fist, in the Name of Jesus.

I break the *spirit of hoarding,* in the Name of Jesus.

I *loose* the *spirit of cleanliness, holiness,* the *spirit of ENOUGH,* and the *spirit of satisfaction* in the LORD, in Jesus' Name.

I bind and cast out the *spirit of disobedience,* in Jesus' Name.

In Jesus' Name, I bind and cast out the *spirit of rebellion* and the *spirit of procrastination,* which all tend to *poverty*.

Where other people are spending money, I refuse to put up a false posture, in the Name of Jesus.

Spirit of pride, spirit of competition I bind you, in the Name of Jesus. I do not care to keep up with the Jones' or compete with them.

Star

My star –my God-given, God-appointed star, ARISE and shine now for your Light has come. My star-- shine, show me favor and lead my divine helpers to me, in the Name of Jesus.

Strongmen

In the Name of Jesus, I have power over the scorpion and the serpent, the young adder, the…great serpent, I bind you, I trample you under foot and I cast you out.

Every stronghold of *physical, emotional, and spiritual poverty* in my life be pulled down by Fire, in the Name of Jesus.

I bind every demon, devil, and strongman placed to enforce any curse against me, especially the *curse of poverty*.

Every stronghold of *poverty* where I live, where I work, I pull you down; I bind your strongman, in Jesus' Name.

I send warrior angels to my house, & workplace to purge, cleanse and remove every unclean spiritual thing. Lord, reveal any physical thing that should be removed from home or work that serves as a point of contact for unclean *spirits*, in Jesus' Name.

You, stronghold of *poverty,* see the Fire of God, in Jesus' Name.

Evil Weapons

I destroy by Fire every weapon of *poverty* targeted against my life, in the Name of Jesus.

Every descendant of *poverty*, every result of *poverty*, in my life, fall down and *die* in the Name of Jesus.

Every evil power sitting on my prosperity, GET UP!, GET OUT!, somersault and die, in the Name of Jesus.

Lose my location, in the Name of Jesus.

I cut myself and my family off from every inherited *poverty,* in the Name of Jesus.

Instead, I inherit all the blessings, all the favor, all the prosperity from my family's bloodline. From the generations of my family. Everything that has been stolen, bound up, kept, kept away, in Jesus' Name.

Father, where appropriate, show us, tell us our REAL *surname* so we may know what the inheritance of that family Name is and receive the blessings of that family Name, in the Name of Jesus I pray.

Spirit of God's favor; angels of God's blessings and favor, locate me now, in the Name of Jesus.

Every stigma of *poverty* in my life be rubbed off by the Blood of Jesus. I break the *spirit of shame* in myself and down my family line. I do not claim it-- I bind it and release it, in Jesus' Name.

Every adjustment to humiliate me, I rebel against you, in the Name of Jesus.

Every power adjusting my life to *poverty,* fall down and die, in the Name of Jesus.

Every wicked weapon fashioned against my life, backfire against the enemy, in the Name of Jesus.

Today I demand sevenfold restitution from Satan, in the Name of Jesus.

Wall of Fire

LORD, put a wall of Fire against me to protect me from all evil, in the Name of JESUS.

I bind every *spirit of retaliation* against me, my family, my house, all things under my stewardship because of these prayers, in the Name of Jesus.

FATHER, heal me of any and all damages of every arrow sent against me in the spirit that I do not have any natural effects because of them, in the Name of JESUS. RETURN all evil arrows back to sender.

Evil agents: Enjoy your arrows; I send them all, speedily back to you, because, clearly, I do not receive them, in the Name of Jesus.

Wealth & Riches

The riches of the Gentiles shall come upon me, in Jesus' Name. The wealth of the wicked is laid up for the just. (Proverbs 13:22)

I retrieve my purse and wallet from Judas and every other thief, in Jesus's Name.

Let there be a reverse transfer of my satanically transferred wealth back to me, in the Name of Jesus.

I take over the wealth of sinners, in Jesus' Name.

I recover the steering wheel of my wealth from the hands of evil drivers; you are not in charge of my life or finances, in the Name of Jesus.

Oh Lord, revive my blessings by Your Fire.

Oh Lord, return my stolen blessings unto me a million-fold.

Oh Lord, send out Your angels, the Angels of God, to bring me blessings.

Whatever needs changing in my life to bring my blessings, be changed by Fire, now, in the Name of Jesus.

Every power that is sitting on my wealth, fall down and die, in the Name of Jesus.

Dear Reader

Thank you for acquiring and reading this book. I pray that you defeat the strongman, the spirit of poverty and live the abundant life that Jesus intended that we have.

Dr. Marlene Miles

Related titles by this author

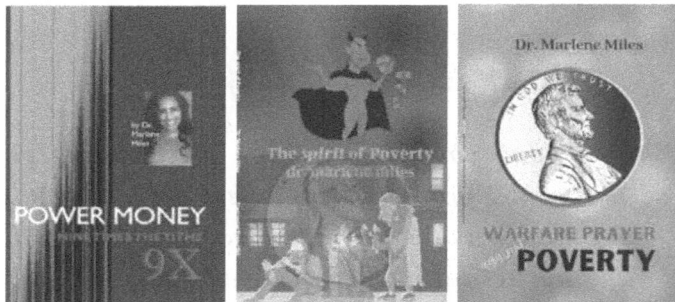

Other books by this author

AK: The Adventures of the Agape Kid

AMONG SOME THIEVES

Churchzilla, *the Wanna-Be, Supposed-to-be Bride of Christ*

Demonic Cobwebs (Prayers Against)

Demons Hate Questions

Don't Refuse Me, Lord (4 book series)

> **Don't Refuse Me, Lord**
>
> **Lord, Help My Debt**
>
> **As My Soul Prospers**
>
> **Do Not Work for Money**

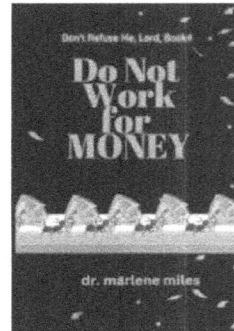

Don't Say That to Me

every apple

The Fold (4 book series)

    The Fold (Book 1)

    Name Your Seed (Book 2)

The Poor Attitudes of Money (Book 3)

Do Not Orphan Your Seed

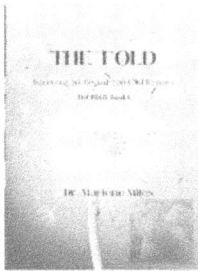

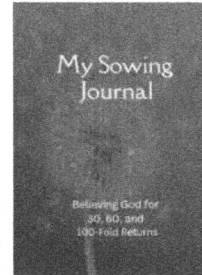

got HEALING? Verses for Life

got LOVE? Verses for Life

got money?

HOW TO DENTAL ASSIST

Let Me Have A Dollar's Worth

Man Safari, *The*

Marriage Ed. *Rules of Engagement & Marriage*

Made Perfect in Love

Power Money: Nine Times the Tithe

The Power of Wealth *(forthcoming)*

Seasons of Grief

Seasons of War

The Spirit of Poverty

Warfare Prayer Against Poverty

When the Devourer is Rebuked

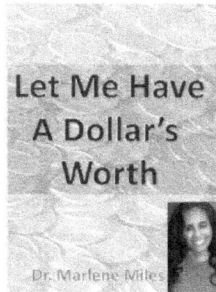

Above are two mini books that explain tithing and sowing in the offering.

When the Devourer is Rebuked describes church life when everyone is tithing and there is not devourer to gobble up anyone's finances.

Let Me Have A Dollar's Worth quickly teaches why you want to sow generously in the offerings.

The Wilderness Romance *(3-book series)*

The Social Wilderness

The Sexual Wilderness

The Spiritual Wilderness

Journals & Devotionals

The Cool of the Day – *Journal for times spent with God*

got Wisdom?

got Grace?

got Joy?

got Peace?

He Hears Us, Prayer Journal *in 4 colors*

***I Have A Star*, Dream Journal** *kids, teen, young adult & up.*

***I Have A Star*, Guided Prayer Journal,** *2 styles: Boy or Girl*

J'ai une Etoile, Journal des Reves

Let Her Dream, Dream Journal *in multiple cover colors*

Men Shall Dream, Dream Journal, *(blue or black)*

My Favorite Prayers *(multiple cover styles)*

My Sowing Journal (in three different colors)

Tengo una Estrella, Diario de Sueños

<u>Illustrated children's books by this author:</u>

Be the Lion (3-book series)

Big Dog (8-book series)

Do Not Say That to Me

Every Apple

Fluff the Clouds

I Love You All Over the World

Imma Dance

The Jump Rope

Kiss the Sun

The Masked Man

Not During a Pandemic

Push the Wind

Slide

Tangled Taffy

What If?

Wiggle, Wiggle; Giggle, Giggle

Worry About Yourself

You Did Not Say Goodbye to Me

Notes:

Notes:

Notes:

www.ingramcontent.com/pod-product-compliance
Lightning Source LLC
Chambersburg PA
CBHW071908020426
42331CB00010B/2711